HEART'S AGONY
SELECTED POEMS OF CHIHA KIM

HEART'S AGONY
SELECTED POEMS

CHIHA KIM

TRANSLATED BY
WON-CHUNG KIM AND JAMES HAN

WHITE PINE PRESS • FREDONIA, NEW YORK

Publication of this book was made possible, in part, by grants
from the National Endowment for the Arts
and the New York State Council on the Arts
and by the Korean Ministry of Culture.

Book design: Elaine LaMattina
Printed and bound in the United States of America

ISBN 1-877727-84-9

9 8 7 6 5 4 3 2 1
Published by White Pine Press
10 Village Square, Fredonia, New York 14063

Library of Congress Cataloging-in-Publication Data

Kim, Chi-ha, 1941–
Heart's agony : selected poems / Chiha Kim ; translated by
Won-Chung Kim and James Han.
p.   cm. — (Human rights series ; v. 5)
Translated from various titles in Korean.
ISBN 1-877727-84-9
I. Kim, Won-jung. II. Han, James. III. Title.
IV. Series: Human rights series (Fredonia, N.Y.) ; v. 5.
PL992.415.C46A255   1998
895.7' 14—dc21   98-15908
                                           CIP

CONTENTS

PREFACE / 9

INTRODUCTION / 15

THE FIRST PART

The Ocher Road / 37
At the Field / 39
Blue Clothes / 41
I Can't See Even Star-light / 42
With a Burning Thirst / 43
Sooyu-ri Diary / 44
In the Darkness / 45
The Night Country / 46
Brook 2 / 47
A Bird / 49
Never Will You Return / 50
Chiri Mountain / 52
Hell 2 / 54
The Empty Mountain / 55
The Rain / 56
No Short Cuts / 58
Something So Obvious / 59
Life / 60
Poetry / 61
A Letter / 62
Let's See Small Things / 63
An Armful of Flowers for the Rusted Locomotive / 64
The Figure of a Horseman / 66

A Wish 1 / 67
A Wish 2 / 68
A Wish 3 / 69
The Sea / 70

THE SECOND PART

Cracking the Shell / 75
Whatever / 76
In the Past / 77
Heart's Agony / 78
New Spring 3 / 79
New Spring 4 / 80
New Spring 6 / 81
New Spring 8 / 82
The Gaps / 83
Respect / 84
Flower-envying Cold 1 / 85
Ilsan Poems 2 / 86
Ilsan Poems 4 / 87
Ilsan Poems 5 / 88
Inner Flesh 1 / 89
Inner Flesh 3 / 90
Nothing / 91
Loneliness / 92
A Memory / 93
Empty Room / 94
My Home / 95
The Sound of Rain / 96
Cricket / 97
Autumn Twilight / 98

A New Church / 99
To the West / 100

THE THIRD PART

Five Thieves / 103

NOTES ON THE POEMS / 126

THE TRANSLATORS / 128

PREFACE

H. D. says in her *Trilogy* that in the midst of air bombings in World War II she saw walls collapsing and a new world so far hidden from man's eye emerging. Chiha Kim of Korea also saw the adamant walls of the military regime, against which he fought with all his body and soul, fall down and a new world open before his eyes. From the very beginning of his poetic career he has aspired to a "real" life in which a man can be faithful to his own ideas and fulfill them freely. But less than ideal circumstances in Korea, especially the forces of the anti-democracy government, did not leave Kim free to pursue his own ideals. Faced with suffocating oppression and relentless persecution, Kim, a man of courage and integrity, determined to fight against the dark reality. In the process of fighting, Kim intuited that what must be rumbled down are not the outer world barriers such as political tyranny and persecution but the walls within the self. Paradoxically, in extreme fear of the walls and ceiling of his prison cell collapsing on him, Kim saw a vision of the "fearful" power of life in a small plant growing in the gap between the bars and the concrete wall. In this world of life, walls are broken and everything transforms and circulates freely, realizing its potential while helping others. This recognition of the powerful will of every living thing dramatically changed Kim from a political poet for freedom and democracy into a poet who sings an inner freedom of a new, cosmic self liberated from the old self. But the path to both kinds of freedom is a hard one, and the intensity of Kim's heart's agony to achieve them in his life and art must be recognized. Kim's early poems mainly depict the agony and struggle of the poet for political freedom and democracy, while his later poems are mostly about his soul's agony to be born again as a new, cosmic self.

His own words about the poet's role help us understand what kind of poet he is:

> I am a poet. And the poet is a man who stands in the midst of the miserable lives of the poor, shares their agony and suffering, and expresses it in poetry. He should give hope to the poor by finding the cause of their unhappiness and trying to remove it and by dreaming a better future and presenting its fruit to them. Hence, we call the true poet the flower of the common people. If he chooses to revolt, it is only because he wants to give a dream to the poor neighbors he loves. Because it is a kind of dream, the revolution he dreams of is a totally unheard, creative vision. Therefore the poet's dream of revolution should be understood not by the mere logic of ideology or law, but only by the autonomous dynamics of the poet's imagination.

A poet of revolution surely is he. But we must take notice of the revolution of which he dreams. His compassion and love for others and his own life philosophy which grew gradually in his poetic career, revolutionized his thought pattern. His eyes turned inward, and he dreamed of a revolution of the mind as well as that of the outside world. He perceived in his mature years that the revolution of the mind must precede that of the world. The new world he aspires to is an open world in which all boundaries are broken and everything is interpenetrable. What he is singing of in his later poetry is this new, cosmic world, which runs on the power of compassion and love. He diagnoses our culture as the culture of killing and presents the culture of *salim* (which means both household and bringing things to life in Korean) as an alternative. Like Gary Snyder, he emphasizes the revolution of the mind as a precondition for participating in the community of the whole creation, and man's responsibility for taking care of the earth. His concern for the ecology and environment and for the fate of human beings is shared by many intellectuals in Korea and will win over readers in the West as well. Transformed into a bird—whose life he envied so much in his dark cell—by "cracking the shell" of the ego and attachments, Kim now freely flies over the boundaries and presents a macro-vision of our lives which lies beyond our micro-detail obsessed mind.

To my knowledge three books of Kim's poetry are translated into English: *Cry of the People and Other Poems*, translated by Nicola Geiger (Tokyo, Japan: Autumn Press, 1974), *The Gold Crowned Jesus and Other Writings*, translated by Choy Sun Kim and Shelley Killen (New York: Orbis Books, 1978), and *The Middle Hour: Selected Poems of Kim Chi Ha* translated by David R. McCann (New York: Human Rights Publishing Co, 1980). Considering that a major change took place in the life of the poet in the later part of the 1980s, these books cannot present the whole picture of Kim's poetic world. By translating both his early poems and later ones, I tried to show a balanced picture of the poet. Part I contains selections from his early poems; Part II from his later ones. Part III contains a translation of "Five Thieves," the most famous *Tamsi*, or talk poem, of Chiha Kim.

This kind of work cannot be done alone and I received much help from others. In preparing the translations, I am most grateful to Professor Chan J. Wu, who helped me in every phase of the work and wrote the introductory essay for this book. I am thankful to Professor James Han, who worked patiently with me, reading the manuscript carefully and improving it greatly. Thanks to Chiha Kim, who kindly allowed me to translate his work. My thanks goes also to the Ministry of Culture, which generously provided the funding for the translation and a subsidy for the publication of this book. As always, my wife, Hyunsuk and my daughter, Lily have been an inspiration.

—Won-Chung Kim

The Danish author Peter Hoeg writes, "understanding is something one does best when one is on the borderline." As an American of Korean ancestry, as one of the countless other second-generation Americans who have precariously straddled the line between cultures, understanding is an inherent birthright. It is a birthright, however, that on many occasions I would have gladly forsaken. Understanding comes at a much later point in life, if at all. At first, there is only confusion and mayhem. If the howling ceases and the clarity comes (and in my case, it has not yet come) it is because one has persevered.

Chiha Kim was also a man caught between two worlds—the Korean military regime where he could not express his thoughts freely and his prison cell where he could express his thoughts only to himself. Kim, however, surely persevered and in doing so, was able to reach a new landscape, as his later poetry attests. Kim serves as an admirable example of how to reach the point of clarity, how to understand one's self.

I am forever grateful to Professor Won-Chung Kim who chose me to be a part of this project and who helped me to understand the poetry and ideals of an important Korean. I am thankful to the students at Konyang University who have helped me immensely in Korea and to Joseph Bates who encouraged me to go to Korea. I cannot thank my family enough for being so caring and understanding. Finally, highest thanks to God who has given me a landscape for which to strive.

—James Han

INTRODUCTION

COSMIC BUDS BURGEONING IN WORDS: CHIHA KIM'S POETICS OF FULL-EMPTINESS

1. From a Burning Thirst to the Sea of Life

The wisdom of the Orient, especially that of Buddhism, teaches one how to appreciate the precious beauty of a lotus blooming in the mud. It urges one not to forget the cosmic nature of one's life, however excruciating life may be. Through this wisdom one can paradoxically find hope in the deepest of despair and ultimately concede that life has meaning. Teachers of this wisdom are innate poets, blessed with the Muse's boundless inspiration. The essence of this blessing is a unique sensibility with which to look through the painful reality of daily existence and invigorate it with a cosmic or god-like spirit. In this sense, a born poet is a blessed person indeed. However, not every poet can be a great poet. As crucial as the Muse's gift is, appropriate circumstances must exist so that the poet's sensibility can bloom fully. It is truly paradoxical that the tree of poetry grows better in a soil of conflict and unhappiness than in a happy and prosperous one. Well-known Third World writers such as Nguggi, Naple and Neruda confirm this paradox.

Chiha Kim of Korea is also one of these writers. He wrote with all his will and palpitating might while standing against the military despotism in Korea, which existed from the 1960s to the 1980s. As a symbol of democracy, his life and poetry have become legendary to Koreans. Born in a barren land, he had to suffer not only physical wounds but endure more painful mental wounds as well. Like the Third World peoples living under tyrannical rule, Koreans at that time were drudging around in an insecure and uncertain existence where death lurked ominously in the background. With their bodies tortured and their mouths gagged, they had to either endure degradation or fight against it. Life was hardly life in the sense that we imagine it but rather was a state closer to death. Those who sought life were forced instead to experience the bitterness of death. Chiha Kim swallowed his cup of bitterness in an unyielding struggle for his life and art. He endured and fought against the surrounding dark reality with a burning thirst, as the title of one of his books suggests. He witnessed cruelty and barbarity in the murders of his compatriots. Sentenced to death himself, he experienced everything that death could possibly mean to a man. But in the nadir of death and alone with his burning thirst, Chiha Kim, surmounted dark reality and reached the "sea of life." Through thirty years of writing poetry, he arrived at a world of nirvana in which the distinctions between life and death break down completely. In this new, open world every creation helps the other to realize life fully through supporting, embracing and interpenetrating each other freely. In short, this world is a "full-empty" universe, a round world of fullness and a world of emptiness perfectly harmonized.

2. Existential Seriousness and Literary Dynamics

Chiha Kim was born in Mokpo City, a seaport located in southern Korea, on February 4, 1941. At that time, Korea was under the control of the Japanese. Kim was born in a colonized land and faced the brutality of the Korean War at the age of nine. As a college student, he participated in the April 19th revolution. This was the beginning of his life-long struggle for democracy. Shortly after, he began a repetitive cycle of being hunted, going into hiding, being arrested and imprisoned. He was first imprisoned in 1964 for fighting against the unpopular agreement that normalized relations between South Korea and Japan. He spent a total of eight years in prison before his final release. In the course of those years, Kim had been given a life sentence and was also sentenced to death. Though the government was constantly suppressing all democratic movements, he never lost his firm belief in democracy or his zeal for poetry. When he published "Five Thieves" in 1970, a bitter and ironic parody of the military regime, high officials and plutocrats, the government threw him in jail on the absurd grounds that he had violated the ban against anti-Communist activity. Though they could bind his body in prison, Kim's unyielding poetic spirit was beyond their control. He never stopped writing "talk poems," dramas and essays that expressed his earnest hope for democracy and "real" human life. In Korea, the public had little access to these works because of the undemocratic forces in power. However, they were published in Japan, where Kim first gained international exposure. When he was sentenced to death in 1974 by the Korean Constitutional Court for violating the emergency code, world-wide efforts to save Kim were begun in Japan. The Asian and African Writers Conference which was held in Moscow on June 29th, 1975, awarded Kim the Lotus Prize, generally regarded as the Third World's Nobel Prize. They also sent

Chunghee Park, the President of Korea at that time, a letter of petition to release Kim. They argued that Kim, in addition to being a symbol of freedom and democracy, was one of the best poets not only in Asia but in the world. Around that time Kim was put forth as a candidate for the Nobel Peace Prize and the Nobel Prize for Literature by writers and intellectuals from Japan, the United States and Europe. Despite these efforts, Kim was destined to spend many more days in his dark cell. He was finally released in 1980 following the assassination of Park and the downfall of his regime, a demise that Kim had predicted.

His second book of poetry, *With a Burning Thirst*, came out in 1982, twelve years after his maiden effort, *The Ocher Road*. It was in the early '80s that Kim introduced his unique "talk poem" style in *The South*. In this talk poem, Kim reveals his philosophy of life, a beautiful blend of Korea's traditional "Tonghak Idea" and the thought patterns of the common man. He continues to systematize his ideals and embody them in his poems, most recently in *Aerin* (1986), *Black Mountain and White Room* (1986), *The Rain Cloud in This Drought* (1986), *Looking Forward to the Starry Field* (1989) and *Heart's Agony* (1994). His poems were published in a comprehensive collection in 1993. His prose includes *Food, The Fisher's Song in the South, From a Burning Thirst to the Sea of Life* and *Life*.

Kim's poetry has usually been discussed and evaluated in a political context due to his activities promoting democracy. His readers, especially foreign readers, showed interest in the political aspects of his poetry rather than in the actual poetic texts. The so-called "Chiha Kim syndrome" of the '70s and '80s must be analyzed against the political backdrop of those decades. However, by the '90s the general opinion about Kim began to change. With the sudden disintegration of the Soviet Union and East Germany and the ensuing changes in world politics, Korea's political situation improved and Kim's poetry began to be studied not because of its political usefulness but because of its literary achievements. This turn was quite natural. His new poetic vision, which had fermented nearly a decade in prison, went above and beyond the mere political dimension. His most recent works advocate the idea that all living things are connected to each other. In this world, nothing stands alone; man is connected to man, man to nature, man to the world, world to the universe. Kim's artistic imagination has intuited this symbiotic universe, a concept with universal appeal.

3. The Poesy of Political Imagination

Chiha Kim's poetic journey begins on the barren ocher road. The political and economic situation in Korea in the '60s and '70s was miserable. It was a thorny age of suffering and struggle, the aftermath of Japanese colonization, the Korean War and the ensuing military regime. As expressed in one of his early poems, "The Ocher Road," the misery of the father's generation is handed down intact to the speaker, the next generation. The speaker suffers the same experience of being dragged away at gun point as the father did. The son laments his father's pains, "Born in an impoverished colony / Father, you, too, have fallen down under guns and swords." The imagery of handcuffs and guns emphasizes the helplessness of life on the ocher road, smeared with blood.

Phrases in the poem such as "the searing sun" and "the long, hot summer / Of cruel tyranny" attest to the wretchedness of their lives. This is the place where growth stops, life is suffocated and hope dries up. In "The Figure of a Horseman" Kim depicts a similar situation where all positive energy and hope and even nothingness freeze:

The frieze of life forces

Of powerful human forces
Of lunging armies
Of rippling radiant muscles,
The dazzling iridescence of dripping sweat,
The steely shouts and cries.
All are frozen under the scorching sun.
The expression, the anger, the courage,
The love, the absence and the full nothingness.

Kim's agony is revealed in this poem, where the forces of grass-roots power, courage and love are all frozen. The oxymoron "the full nothingness" is a statement not only of an unyielding spirit of resistance but also of keen perception. Kim's spirit revolts against the political tyranny that deprives man of basic human rights.

The dialectic of "oppression-imprisonment-release" and of "lock and key" in his political poems calls for special attention. His most famous early poems such as "Blue Clothes," "Never Will You Return," and "In the Darkness" are all deeply related to his own experience in prison. "In a strange village at night in this dark age / Being unable to endure it / Without fighting and hurting each other," he laments that he "can't see even starlight." ("I Can't Even See Starlight"). The political situation and his imprisonment caused Kim to feel a dual bitterness, with his poems being his only refuge. In this respect, "Blue Clothes," which graphically depicts the cruel fate of the prisoner and his earnest hope for freedom, is a masterpiece that elicits tears:

Oh! If a morning glory and sunbeam rested
On my bright tear-brimming eyes
That have, through the dark night, waited
For the dawn with a gut-wrenching pain
What a blessing it would be!

Oh! If I could stand even for a minute under
the showering sun
Emerging in the blue sky from the black clouds,
What a blessing it would be even to die dressed
in these blue clothes!

The image of "the bright morning glory" contrasts sharply with "the black cloud" and "blue sky." However, the "blues" found throughout the poem do not symbolize the same ideas. Consider the contrast between "the blue sky" and "the morning glory" with that of "the blue clothes." While the natural blue of the sky and the morning glory symbolizes man's true hope and his desire for freedom, the man-made blue of the prison uniform stands for repression and the wretchedness of despair. When the repressive blue strangles one's body and soul, hope changes into a pathos of anger. Hence, the angry repetition of "Man is not an animal / Man is not an animal / Man is not an animal" in "Brook 2." The anger leads him to a state of "burning thirst" in which the poet cries "Long Live Democracy" "In tears, subduing the crying sound":

In the back alley at daybreak
I write your name, O Democracy.
My mind has forgotten you for too long
And my legs far too long have strayed from you.
But with a slender remembrance of
My heart's burning thirst,
Secretly I write your name.

In this poem, sung by many Koreans who had hoped for freedom and democracy, we notice the poet's earnest wish for a new world of liberation. But the real situation is one of complete deadlock. The closed iron gate to his cell denies any physical escape. It is the poet's imagination that offers some release. The most notable example of this yearning to be free is found in the bird motif, frequently appearing in his political poems. "Blue Clothes" begins with his hope, "I wish I were a bird," and the symbolism in "A Bird" is fairly obvious:

> Why does clear, clean sky
> And white clouds over a shining mountain
> Make me cry?
> Flying Bird!

> Though I gnaw on
> My imprisoned heart all through the night
> The inner longing of my flesh remains untouched
> And only my blood,
> The rotten blood of summer, drips.

The contrast between the bird flying freely over the shining mountains and the "imprisoned heart" which drips "the rotten blood of summer" effectively conveys the inner as well as the outer landscape. In losing everything, only "the inner longing of flesh remains untouched." Only this longing allows him to endure his situation. The intensity of the longing is utilized as a weapon with which he can fight against corrupt politics. On a poetic level, the longing sublimates his pathos into a tragic lyricism. The political context of Kim's poetry is based on the dialectical conflict and tension between the anti-democratic situation of the outside world and his inner aspiration for freedom. Sometimes directly and sometimes symbolically, his poetic epistemology insists that every living thing should be liberated from oppression, imprisonment, binding, suffocation, hunger and pain and brought into the new horizon of full life. This type of political mes-

He bribes ministers
and buys out vice-ministers
and handles them easily as a cook kneading dough.
His favorite dishes are tax money, foreign loans,
...

By offering his numerous daughters
as concubines to the men holding swords,
he easily winnows out top secrets.
Therefore all the best deals end up in his lap.
With only a $5 million bid he steals
something worth $1 billion.

The second thief is a senator who has been elected through a corrupt election and is mad about making money by any means; he gladly changes national laws to suit his purposes. Kim parodies the corrupt official, the third thief, by writing, "His way is to say 'No, by no means' to realistic projects / and 'Yes, no problem' to impossible ones. / On his desk lie huge files of paper / and under the desk lie bundles of bank notes. / He is a spaniel to his superiors and / a hound to his inferiors. / He makes a fortune by embezzling official money / and by openly asking for bribes." The fourth, a general, and the fifth, a minister are not unlike the first three. Kim criticizes them less for not taking care of the people, but more for madly pursuing their own interests and pleasures. The behavior patterns of the five thieves reflect the political and economic situation of the time. The military regime repressed the basic rights of the individual in the name of modernization while at the same time it protected the rights of a privileged few. Kim fully uses the traditional rhetorical devices and figures of *Pansori* in parodying the five thieves. Literary techniques such as catalogue, repetition, contrast, parallelism, personification and hyperbole are adroitly employed to heighten the ironic effect of the poem. By avoiding direct attacks on the five thieves and relying more on irony and parody, Kim achieves his intended result more effectively.

Readers should note the dual function of laughter in this poem. On the one hand, it is a mask for hiding scathing criticism, while on the other hand it is enveloped by the pathos of crying. Kesoo's ultimate fate in "Five Thieves" is a good example of the latter use of laughter. The plaintive tone describing Kesoo speaks not only of the tragic life of the common people, but also criticizes the five thieves as being the very cause of the people's unhappiness. By skillfully controlling his distance, the speaker can successfully convey tragic sublimity:

> It is twilight,
> and the sun is sinking in the West,
> adding to the life-farer's loneliness.
> A single goose looks for her companion
> under the white, crescent moon,
> and the river bleeds in the crimson twilight.
> While a cuckoo cries and wails sadly,
> the police chief burps and limps,
> dragging Kesoo, dwindled to the size of a pea.
> Alas, Alas!
> Poor and miserable Kesoo,
> my Kesoo,
> You came to Seoul to earn a living,
> unable to live in Chulla-do,
> and you suffered every oppression and ill-treatment
> in an unforgiving Seoul wherever you went.
> What a nice destination

jail is for you!
But Alas!
What can we do,
and who can stand up for you and deliver you
from such an unfair and ridiculous plight!
Farewell, Kesoo,
good-bye Kesoo,
please take care.

After "Five Thieves," Kim continued to criticize Korea's political situation in the '70s in talk poems such as "Nonsense," "Five Acts" and "Sea of Dung." It was a time when the poet himself felt cornered tightly: criticize or commit suicide. This parodic vein in Tamsi was a survival technique in a dark age of oppression. At that time, it was the only way to maintain both political and literary standard simultaneously. The world of Kim's Tamsi expands into a wider and bigger world—the sea of life or the universe of Buddha.

5. Interconnection and the New Buds of the Cosmic Tree

If the political intent and strategy are too intense in a poem, the poem can be seen as a form of weapon. This holds true for Kim's *Tamsi*. However, in the '80s, Kim found another poetic realm. "A Wish 1" is a good example demonstrating the shift in Kim's philosophy and aesthetic sense:

When I
Unsheathe my sword
Oh, that it would change into
A lotus flower.

Though my body is all bloody
And I may die in the deadly battle
Let what I hold
Be not a sword
But a lotus flower.

The change from the world of "sword" to one of "lotus" is extremely significant. While a sword is a military and political weapon, a symbol of conflict, opposition and division, the lotus is a life-giving cosmic flower, a traditional symbol of the blessed state in which every living thing enjoys a harmonious relationship. Kim explains how he is led to this new lotus vision:

Around that time I saw the dust filling the small gaps between the concrete wall and iron bars. The plant seeds, getting moisture from rain, were starting to sprout in those gaps. A wonder it was. I once noticed on a spring day a dandelion-seed tuft moving through the iron bars freely, dancing into the room. It was beautiful indeed. On my way outside to exercise, I even noticed many unfamiliar flower buds abloom on the red bricks of the prison.

How bitterly I wept in my cell that day! How powerful and fresh that one word—life. It held me! Before the one great life that fills the infinite universe and before the unending stream of life, there can be neither wall nor division, nor decay nor death. The more I thought it over, the smaller I felt myself, and at last I seemed to be no bigger than a grain of millet. My heart seemed to contract and my psyche divided. I wondered how I could teach my body and soul this principle of life and make it my own.

I came to the realization that life and death, affirmation

and negation coexist and move back and forth from one
pole to the other continuously.

(*From a Burning Thirst to the Sea of Life*)

This intuition of the meaning of life was a pivotal point in Kim's
career as a poet. This new paradigm of life results from his having
experienced the extremities of life and death. He diagnoses the pre-
sent as the age in which everybody's life is being destroyed daily.
Explaining that life is a key word in leading people to recognize the
importance of the problem, Kim argues for the urgency of recovering
the essential nature of life, which is boundless, free and creative and
always changing while creating harmony.

Kim's compassion reaches to every living thing; he hopes that they
recover their own essential nature while creatively changing and uni-
fying themselves. His boundless compassion for damaged and injured
life is well expressed in *Aerin*, a serial poem. If Kim expresses his sym-
pathy and love for all creation in *Aerin*, he sings of rebirth and new
life in *Heart's Agony*. This is a noteworthy change, one that demon-
strates Kim's insight into his own life and literature even at the rela-
tively late age of fifty. In the Orient, the age of fifty is generally regarded
as the age when one can discover heaven's will. In the preface of the
book Kim is saying that he wants to enjoy the agony of getting out of
his ego through the gaps and spreading true life through the numer-
ous meshes of Indra's net. This desire is a result of his intuition of
heaven's will. But to escape through the net is just as difficult as intu-
iting heaven's will. It requires many nights of agony and sleeplessness.

What is the landscape of the life that Kim perceives in his vision?
In short, it is a boundless, open world in which each creation changes
its shape freely while helping others to fulfill their dreams. It is a
world where mutual living is actualized and reversible reaction is pos-
sible:

I hear
The rain
Which falls from the sky and
Soars on back, after traveling to the earth.

("The Sound of Rain")

As the poems show, life and death, descent and ascent, closedness
and openness are not separate entities but are organically connected
in the poet's imagination. Kim's marvelous vision of the new life in
which he deconstructs all distinction, reverses all positions and
widens all gaps so that all life can penetrate one another is not much
different from the cosmic principle of mutual living by transforma-
tion. "Cracking the Shell" is one of his best poems embodying this
idea:

At evening,
A green star burns
Within my loins.
It rises above my navel
Into my skull.

I am burnt hollow
And now a tree grows in me.

Dead and transformed
Into a crescent moon
I rise over the trees.

Love,
Let me know
The mystic hour of birth.

I'll break my shell
Kick through
To be born again
As the Universe.

Kim's intuition of the organic transformation of body-tree-moon-body tells us of the eternity of one's life and the fact that eternity is nowhere but in our body. The poems clearly show Kim's poetic epistemology. Terms such as "new birth," "love" and "resurrection" indicate that Kim is pursuing a life in which the cosmic principle is fully actualized based on the realization of the interconnectedness of every living thing. This is a great change indeed for Kim who had once encouraged a spirit of revolt. Now, the poet says, "My heart leaps / At the wonder of all living things" ("New Spring 6"). "Love / Cosmic and unknown / Shoots out like the wind / From my empty heart" ("Nothing"). Having experienced this love, the poet can clearly see "The bud of the cosmos / Shoots everywhere" ("Respect").

The landscape of the new life beyond the death-infected present is similar to the sea of Buddha, where cosmic buds shoot out in the spring and every living thing helps the other, thereby attaining a state of harmony. The poet, who is singing "the song of myself" in the sea of life or in the open world, is a shaman of the full-empty universe. The shaman presents the world of great affirmation by humiliating himself before and showing respect to the cosmic life. Kim's later poetry, which had come forth of a weary body and soul that had experienced repression, imprisonment and sickness, is comparable to a cosmic tree which never stops sending out new shoots. They are the shoots of a cosmic sound and a new life.

6. *The Poetic Career of Chiha Kim and Its Meaning*

The poetic career of Kim is varied and rather unusual. For thirty years, Kim wrote poetry in which he tried to harmonize his political and literary lives; this is a history in and of itself. At the same time, these thirty years are a contemporary history of Korea and, in a sense, of the world. His poetic journey from "The Ocher Road" to "Five Thieves" to "Cracking the Shell" leaves us with several points to consider and ponder.

First, his life philosophy changes from the realm of the political imagination to the ecological imagination. While the former relies heavily on a world view of binary opposition, the latter stems from a view of a cyclical and circular universe. His political imagination shows a pathos of confrontation, revolt, criticism and satire; his ecological imagination is one of compassion, interconnection, love, embrace, respect and transformation. This shift is representative of the change in thinking in Korean society in the latter half of the Twentieth century and accords with the present worldwide concern for nature and the environment.

Second, the journey shows continuity. His lifelong poetic theme of "the interconnectedness of all life" runs as an undercurrent beneath the enormous change. The pathos in both his early poems and later poems stem from his unbending belief in the innate worth of every living thing. His life philosophy shows a mature form in the '80s, the result of decades of building. However, his early poems reveal early signs of the philosophy which would come to be.

Third, his constant agony and struggle for creating a new poetic form, his self-consciousness about poetry, his profound meditation on the relationship between politics and poetics and between the universe and poetry must be appreciated. His talk poems, most notably "Five Thieves," were an important force in the modernization of a traditional literary genre.

Fourth, although his ideas on freedom, democracy, liberation and life grew out of Korean soil, they are, I think, applicable to other Third World writers. In this respect, Kim is one of the best poets that not only Korea but the world has produced.

Finally, his life philosophy and literary works are a meaningful landscape for the end of the Twentieth Century. His philosophy embraces and offers potential solutions to problems encompassing gender, race, environmental contamination, labor, alienation and mental illness. It will surely position itself as one of the most inclusive and original philosophies, capable of integrating man and universe, man and man, man and nature in a discontinuous continuity.

—Chan J. Wu
Literary critic
Professor of Korean Literature,
Sogang University

The First Part

THE OCHER ROAD[1]

I follow you, father,
Your translucent trail of blood
On the ocher road.
You are dead
And now the sun burns black.
I follow you into the summer heat of guns and swords
With handcuffs on both wrists
Where the searing sun
Burns away sweat, tears, and fields of rye.
I follow you, father
To Puzu Cape where gray fish leap,
Where you died wrapped in a burlap sack.
I follow after you, father

When Opo Mountain brightens at night with fire,
When sun shines on the yellow road
Making the tender orange leaves of the trifoliate hedge as sharp
And stiff as the fully-grown leaves,
Shall I shout
Or sing a song?

Every ten years blood bubbles up in the wells
Of Hwadang village, where bamboo fences decay.[2]
Born in an impoverished colony,
Father, you too have fallen down under guns and swords.
How could the water drops welling in the bamboo shoots
Not know that crystal-clear May is coming?

In the long, hot summer
Of cruel tyranny, in which small cockles
Were starved to death and heaven hid its face
All the days and hope
Of my country
Were forced in the end onto the dusty yellow road

Across the slime in which an old
Boat lies broken by age and sun,
The blue sky hangs high
Over white-furrowed fields of rye.
Despite ten long years,
The shouting that shook the sky that day
Revives in my breath
And in my body, steel wires tense.

Sensing your voice
I follow you with tears, father,
To where you died,
To Puzu Cape where gray fish leap,
Where you died wrapped in a burlap sack.

AT THE FIELD

What
Crumbles around me?
What is that shouting
At Hantan-ri field where the wind's beautiful white ripples
Kiss the sun-warmed ground?
What is it that crumbles
Little by little?

As if dreaming a terrible dream of old war sites
The sun shudders with fear.
Several gunshots ring
Over sun-bleached heaps of stone.
The wind whispers softly.

It is the sound of
Old mountain ridges breaking apart
And the shouting of flowers and
wild strawberries ripening madly
On an old crumbled castle-keep.
It is the sound of a brass trumpet
Signalling the long strife
Between fading powers and emerging ones
And the sound of my blood boiling
Reverberates my ears
And in my heart

When I stand
In the desolate field where irises are burning

Softly and steadily like an advancing evening tide
I hear the crumbling sounds again and again,
The sound of something crumbling
Little by little.

BLUE CLOTHES[3]

I wish I were a bird
Or the water or the wind

Instead of being in blue clothes which wrap
My naked lean body
I would wear the sea for a while in a dream

My heart bleeds with pain, pierced by
The square red patch.[4]
Oh! if I could tear it off
And live without it,
I would gladly die
And suffer the fate of dust scattered to the winds

Oh! if a morning glory and sunbeam rested
On my bright tear-brimming eyes
That have, through the dark night, waited
For the dawn with a gut-wrenching pain
What a blessing it would be!

Oh! if I could stand even for a minute under the showering sun
Emerging in the blue sky from the black clouds,
What a blessing it would be even to die dressed in these blue clothes!

Oh! if it were real,
Right here and now
Never to be covered again
And again.

I Can't See Even Starlight

After vomiting everything
With a cry I rise
And look up at the sky
Leaning against the still warm, crumbling mud wall.

Unable to bear the situation without hurting each other,
Afraid they will go mad,
My miserable friends drink in the half-lit room
Where there is absolutely nothing,
Not even wind to rustle a bamboo leaf,
Where only emptiness
And dryness dwell.

This farewell drinking party is for
You who will pass over Ginburyung
And fish for cuttle at Kangneung
And me who will find refuge in some mine
At daybreak.

In a strange village at night in this dark age
Being unable to endure it
Without fighting and hurting each other,
I lean against the mud wall and look up at the sky,
And I can't see even starlight.

WITH A BURNING THIRST

In the back alley at daybreak
I write your name, O Democracy
My mind has forgotten you for too long
And my legs far too long have strayed from you.
But with a slender remembrance of
My heart's burning thirst,
Secretly I write your name.

Somewhere in the back alley before dawn
The rush of footsteps, urgent whistles, and pounding,
Someone's long, unending shriek,
Someone's groan, wail, lament
find their way into my heart,
Engraving themselves there.
For your name's sake,
For the solitary splendor of your name,
On a wooden board with white chalk
I write awkwardly with shaking hand, trembling heart
And raging indignation
The agony of living
The memory of green freedom reviving
And the blood-stained faces of returning friends
Who'd been taken by the police

I write your name secretly
In tears, subduing the crying
With a burning thirst
With a burning thirst
Long live Democracy!

SOOYU-RI DIARY

For whose neck is this silk noose?
The long white hand touches
My forehead night after night.

Every mountain ridge that swells with
Full-blossom lilies in the wind
Runs wild with crimson brooks.

The moon rises only
On the worn-out Whatu[5]
And slides down, in a drunk-red stupor.

My life has been mere shadow,
a humped shadow
Flickering on the mud wall in kerosene-lamp light.
Even strong Soju[6] can't assuage my anger
But, instead, burns my heart,
Inflaming it again

Mountains!
Rise lightly over the clouds.
Red lamplight and white baby moon!
Rise high smoothly over the sky.
Cabbage head! dance and sing
Until early dawn strides back along with the wind.

While rock salt breaks with a bang between molars
And wild dogs keep barking in a distant forest unseen,
Every mountain brook runs blood-red
And my heart still burns,
Burns red and white again and again.

IN THE DARKNESS

Someone calls to me
In the darkness,
From the iron bars of the cell across from mine.
The darkness is rusty red.
Two glowing eyes in that darkness
Call silently to me.
Phlegmy breathing calls to me.

Someone calls to me
On this day when rain sprinkles softly from the low grey sky
Though the sounds of doves cooing on the roof,
The sounds of keys, trumpets, and footsteps
Drown the calls frequently,
Somebody calls to me again and again
Blood-stained, worn out underwear hanging from the windowsill,
The crimson souls writhing so many nights in their cells,
And the cries of mangled bodies
All call to me and my blood
With their soft silence.
With a shake of their heads
They protest
And deny all the lies.

On a day when the rain sprinkles softly
From the low grey sky
Two glowing open eyes
call to my raw, naked body
In the darkness.

NIGHT COUNTRY

Night is the country of sounds
Soft, shrill, and fading.
Invincible sounds where leaps and bounds of the heart
begin to ease.
Ah! it is a country with no boundaries
And infinite sounds.

Everything alive is dancing
Sadly, miserably, endlessly.
It is a country
Where you are awakend by cold dew
And the gong of an iron drum.
Left at dawn without any destination
It is a country to which, once you die,
Your soul can never return
Though your white-haired head enjoys
The happy sound of heavenly springs

The small pink feet of a baby
Dancing lightly to the sound of a spring
And my memory of kissing you
Are now drowned by the silence of the scorching day
Leaving me with only a suffocating thirst
In which I am fated to die
Crying and raving mad.

BROOK 2

Last night he came
Only to be taken by the police at early dawn.
He left me to cherish the sound of budding flowers
And a running brook beneath last night's lantern light,
He left his burning eyes,
His cries and screams
While being dragged away:
"Man is not an animal!"

The sun-bleached mud walls cried.
The hills, the winding roads,
And the wild azaleas in the mountains
Whose snow melts in my bosom
Cried
Cried
Cried.

My tears gather into a flame
And his screams into a brook.
The brook shouts again and again
And becomes a rolling sea,
A tempest and finally thunder
Which breaks mountain ridges apart.
Ah!
"Man is not an animal!"
"Man is not an animal!"
"Man is not an animal!"

Every brook shouts
As it runs through the fields,
But there is a brook of man's shouting
That grows louder as other brooks fall asleep:
"Man is not an animal!"

A BIRD

Why do clear, clean sky
And white clouds over a shining mountain
Make me cry?
Flying Bird!

Though I gnaw on
My imprisoned heart all through the night ,
The inner longing of my flesh remains untouched
And only my blood,
The rotten blood of summer, drips

My body crawls on the earth
And my sad eyes weep even in daytime.
Thinking of you,
I wish they would disappear.
Bird! end my naked body's struggles,
The unending sound of cold chains!
How can I die and become like you?

The bird flies away
Through slats of sun
Which slowly weaken in my dark spirit
Even as the days grow more bright.

The bird flies over the clear sky's edge,
Passing the blue mountains.
I don't know why it makes me cry.
The boundless bright clouds are fleeting
But my heart is still bound.

NEVER WILL YOU RETURN

Never will you return
Once you fall asleep
In this white room.
This sleep numbs the entire body,
Attacks with a fathomless dizziness

Never will you return
Once you fall asleep
In this white room
To the rough road of life
Though the echoes of moans horrify
And crimson blood stains on the walls
Startle at midnight.

From this room
Where the sound of heeled boots on the ceiling
Never ceases throughout the night,
Strange faces, hands, and gestures
Mock you freely,
Attack with a fathomless dizziness

If I cry, eyes glaring, and endure the pain
Of fingernails plucked out and flesh ripped apart
Can my shriveled soul survive
And stand on the road again?

Many of my friends
Fell into that shameful sleep

And regretfully passed away,
The very friends
Who were so good to me,
Sharing smiles as well as tears

Ah! Never, never will you return
If you fall asleep in this room,
If you don't struggle
With all your might and naked body
To the rough, windy road,
to your brothers,
And to life

CHIRI MOUNTAIN

The sight of the snow-covered mountain
Makes my blood boil.
Green bamboo shoots
Inflame my heart.
Under bamboo trees
Under the mountain
Crimsom blood still runs

Blood still runs
Through every field
And every mountain ridge.
It is a banner
That still cries loudly, testifies to the splendor
Of pure souls who departed with burning eyes

They departed
Leaving behind only a rusted sickle, miserable poverty
And the empty promise of returning alive.
Though they vanished,
Like water trickling under a frozen brook
They came back
And like an unforgettable old song
Still cry in my mind
And pound in my restless heart.

The sight of the snow-covered mountain
Makes my blood boil.
Green bamboo shoots

Inflame my heart
You, still alive, reverberate in my mind.
Oh! Chiri Mountain,
Chiri Mountain.

HELL 2

Nothing
Can you believe here,
Neither the Christ of the masses
Nor your trifling resolution to shave your beard today
Nobody can you believe here
In these dangerous streets
Where lifeless dust nests in the bosom silently,
Rocks grow from clasped hands,
And your bloodshot eyes never blink.

Dry thunder from thick grey clouds
Slowly approaches these streets,
And in these dangerous streets
All things are struck dead
By the sound of machines
And the silence of leafless trees.
Here, unless you wear gloves,
You cannot even hold another's hands
Because they become daggers in your palm.

Dust falls on your chest
And silently petrifies
In these dry November streets
Where only your protesting, mysterious eyes glow.
Oh! these silent streets.

THE EMPTY MOUNTAIN

No one
Climbs the empty mountain
Anymore

On the lonely naked mountain
The sun and wind collide and wail
But after we are gone to dust
Even a hearse can't take us away
From the empty mountain.

Too wearying and hard
Is the day's struggle.
Who can know
If today's embers are tomorrow's flames,
Burning hidden now
Deep within the silent mountain.

Holding a handful of dust
You wail
Beside the mountain you 'll return to
After many deaths

Tomorrow,
You will be a flame
Or a fresh green pine.

THE RAIN

A bird,
A small bird,
Alights on a white hollyhock
On a dish,
And on a dull knife blade

The man who was arrested
Somewhere,
Did he listen carefully
To the sound of
Footsteps scraping against barley leaves
In the far sky?
Has the bound man
Crossed the hill yet?

Why do tears fall
And become drops of blood?
A paper bird
Alights on a hollyhock
And dies there, unable to fly.
Why can't the man fly freely,
Even after death?

A bird
Alights deftly
On the knife blade
A bird with small, red eyes
Alights not only on the flowers in the garden

But also on the flowers in my eyes
Which tear up again
Even after so many tears.

A rain
Of white
Paper
Descends,
Trembling like the curse of the old,
And piles
On the hollyhocks.

SHORT CUTS

Thoughts of escaping this road
Where all is pain,
Wishes of making an end of it on this road
Where meager applause is sometimes heard
Spring from the well of my dark heart.
Halting my awkward steps along the way,
I think
I have to stay on one road,
Though roads are open everywhere

No more attachments,
No more short cuts.

SOMETHING SO OBVIOUS

Forward is not the only way.
Backward is a direction, too.

Ahead and behind,
Around and straight
Are all ways
Of their own.

And only when we know this truth
Can we say
We know how to walk life's way.

In truth we walk
Back and forth on one road
Throughout our lives.

LIFE

Life is
A ray of hope.
My life depends on it
As I stand here at the edge of
An abyss.

I cannot go back
Or forward.

This is the final stop for me.
I can neither soar
Nor fall

A mother cries
And embraces her child.
The sorrow of life
Breeds a ray of hope.

POETRY

When poetry came to me
I spat at it,
And when it tried to leave
I clung to it, saying "You are beautiful."

When poetry hesitated
I said, "Leave me, if you want"
In a small but arrogant voice.

"Leave me, friend."
That's still what I mean.
There is no other way

I asked it to leave me
Though I knew that once gone,
It would never visit me again.
In truth, I said the words
Again and again
Because I was afraid of its returning.

Poetry never comes to me
Though I sit awake the whole night in the prison.
Oh! my friends, I am now thirty-three,
The age when corruption sets in easily,
But there is no other way
Than to say "Leave me, if you want."

A LETTER

Friends
Don't look for me,
The diseased me,
In the heavy snow

Apricot buds!
If you want to stay,
Stay very fragrantly
Camellias!
If you want to bloom,
Bloom bright red
In the heavy snow.

Friends! Let us meet in warm March,
Having lived through snowy winter.
Let us meet casually,
Bloom in lonely fields,
Our refreshing scents,
Scattered by March wind.

Ask for me there.
Don't look for me, .
The diseased me,
In the heavy snow

LET'S SEE SMALL THINGS

The crocodile is a predator,
Huge and carnivorous,
But as in other animals,
There are gaps between his teeth.
Without the commensal birds
Who peck out bits stuck in the gaps,
The crocodile's teeth would decay
And with rotted teeth
His life as a carnivore would be over.

But nature is wise and merciful,
And with her symbiotic principle,
Harmonizes all creations.
Hence crocodile birds.
Just one one-hundredth the size of the crocodile,
But unless they peck out the bits
The crocodile's teeth would soon decay,
And once the teeth began to rot away,
His life as a carnivore would be over.
He would die of hunger

Behold!
The crocodile is great
But greatness is not everything.
Why can't you see the crocodile birds
Who keep the crocodile as he is?
It's time to turn our eyes
From the crocodile to the crocodile birds,
The very birds which show us
The beautiful harmony of nature.

AN ARMFUL OF FLOWERS FOR THE RUSTED LOCOMOTIVE

If you could come to me
Holding an armful of full-blossomed lilies
And mountain azaleas,
If you could come to me
With bright smiles more precious than flowers,
And If I could go out and meet you
And tearfully embrace
Your flowers and smiles
Rather than your thoughts and beliefs,
I would not need to travel
From Wonju to Haenam, from Haenam to Wonju,
From the North to the South and from the South to the North.
The old outdated coal-fueled car,
The rusted locomotive,
Is now a curiosity to schoolboys.
That car
Used to run the Kyongeu line,
Now cut in half by the demarcation line
If I could ride on the train and come to you,
I would fill the car
With green camelia leaves, shining citrons,
Fragrant gardenias, and fig blossoms
And meet you, the bright smile on my plain face
As broad as a full moon and as beautiful as peonies.
Standing again on Wonju street amidst falling snow
Waiting to go back to the South,
I watch the rushing taxis on the streets
And think of the locomotive, still as a rock

On the severed track of the Kyongeu line
And of the loneliness of my people,
Whom the train never carries.
I pour a cup of Soju on the earth as an offering.
Oh! Flowers
When is the time for your glory!

THE FIGURE OF A HORSEMAN

The frieze of life forces,
Of powerful human forces,
Of lunging armies,
Of rippling radiant muscles,
The dazzling iridescence of dripping sweat,
The steely shouts and cries,
All are frozen under the scorching sun.
The expression, the anger, the courage,
The love, the absence, and the full nothingness.
But the figure cracks as the frieze thaws
Until it becomes supple, like a baby, with age

It struggles to move
And a smile spreads on its mouth,
The joy of the flesh, of living flesh, pulsates.
It tries to make a sound,
And the horse is about to whinny.
The legs move and the mane flies at last.
But, ah, is this mere illusion
Caused by the rays
of a blinding sun,
Or an illusion caused by the winds
Warm April wind?

A WISH 1

When I
Unsheathe my sword,
Oh, that it would change into
A lotus flower.

Though my body is all bloody
And I may die in deadly battle,
Let what I grip
Be not a sword
But a lotus flower

Let the half-destroyed stone buddha
Smile at my dead body,
Lying sideways beside it.
Let it laugh heartily.

Ah! Ah! Ah!
How broad is his heart!

A Wish 2

This is no place to stay
But my heart wishes to remain.
I don't know why the bamboo leaves,
With their secret longings, rustle in the snow-covered field
When all desire has disappeared

There is no one to visit me,
So I idle away my days and nights.
I don't know why my front door creaks
With every wind
When my calendar is empty.

Hope comes unannounced
And disappears after whetting my heart's thirst.

To meet new, unfamiliar days,
I climb the long, steep mountainside
Desperately, running out of breath.

Now
Freely sing a song in me,
You who calls me
From afar.

A Wish 3

With wings attached
To my great stone body
I will soar high and fly to heaven.

Out of the dark
And sunless marsh,
Cherishing all remorse,
I will soar in the end.

Today the sun is streaming
And the wind wildly blows.
My whole body cries,
Sinking with every step,
And my hair screams.

"Burn, burst splendidly
Into golden flames,
All things as you are.
Burn fiercely all over the world,
Here and now,
Where the sun is streaming
And the wind wildly blows."

THE SEA

Now I'll go
To the sea.
I'll go any way I can
To the sea which beckons me
With its huge waves.
To the boundless sea
I'll go.

There's no way
To stop the crying
On the black mountain and in this white room
Unless I leave
In a dream of reaching the eternal sea.
But nothing is possible here.

I'll go
To the sea.
Without dreaming of
A boundless world
Bigger than the universe,
Bigger than heaven,
Even the small worm
Cannot be awakened.

Now I'll go
To the sea,
Following old friends
Who were disillusioned,

Destroyed mercilessly,
Possessed by the iridescent dream of Utopia
Enchanted by the submerged Ieo island
Which shows its splendid self on sunny days.

I'll go to the sea
From Baikbang harbor,
From Mooreung valley,
Even from the end of Aogi,
Holding a red camellia
Not yet full-blossomed
Between my lips.
Even if there is no boat
I'll go by any means,
Not alone
But only with you.

On the morning when the sea
Calls and yells to me
Filled with the sound of dewdrops
I'll stand up
And go to the sea
With you.
I'll go while I'm alive
Or my soul will go after death.
Ah, to the sea
which boils with life,
To the boundless, vast home of lives beyond the sea,
To the eternal sea of enlightenment

I'll never go
Alone.
I'll never go
Without you
Even if it's a heaven bigger than the sea,
Or a Universe bigger than the heaven,
Or an eternal sea of enlightenment,
Or the Pure Land.

THE SECOND PART

CRACKING THE SHELL

At evening
A green star burns
In my loins.
It rises above my navel
Into my skull.

I'm burnt hollow
And now a tree grows in me.

Dead and transformed
Into a crescent moon
I rise over the trees.

Love,
Let me know
The mystic hour of birth.

I ll break my shell,
Kick through
To be born again
As the Universe.

WHATEVER

Any
Sound is welcome,
However small.

Lonely
As I am,
I'll not decline
Even a bug-bite,
Utter solitude.

At the-end of
My thoughts,
Sudden illumination blazes.

My life is not simple
But a vast universe
Where every bug and every sound lives and leaps.

A bitter
Laugh,

And then
A Smile.

I bow with respect
To the withered tree outside

And a leaf
Falls down like a prayer.

IN THE PAST

All the confusing thoughts from the past
Have vanished without a trace,

And in that empty space
The shadow of a withered tree lives.

Birds!
Make your nest here

And sing
New songs not yet heard,
A song of
Barley ripening green
With winter deepening,
A song of plum blossoms
And another of red
Camellias.

And, above all, the song of myself
Not the old self but my self newly-born.

HEART'S AGONY

In the spring
I see
A flower stalk shaking.

Centrifugal power
Pushes it up
Through the ground,
Forcing the flower to open
And scatter its seeds
In every direction.

The stalk agonizes
And labors.

I shake also

Tomorrow
I'll go to the country
To
Bare myself and bloom.

NEW SPRING 3

I've been lonely
All through the winter.

Spring has come blissfully to talk
With the grass
And the new shoots.

It teaches me that loneliness is sheer delusion.
Earth, Air, Water, and Wind
Are my brothers,
My elders in fact.
Their words make me happy again

A bird's song,
Like a benediction,
Hovers over my head.

New Spring 4

I'm thankful
That I'm still alive.

More thankful
That I can enjoy
Three meals a day.

Much more thankful
That I can appreciate
Spring flowers again.

I hold the universe
In my placid heart.

Somewhere under the tree
I hear the budding sound of life
And a bird's song.

NEW SPRING 6

Bees
Visit flowers,

And children
Play in the park.

These are too much for me
And my heart leaps
At the wonder of all living things.

NEW SPRING 8

I wonder
How old I really am.

It's three and a half billion years
Since the beginning of life on earth,
Fifteen billion years
Since the eruption of the cosmos,
And an eternity
Before and after that.

Ah! Eternity

In spite of a thousand deaths
My life is undying.

Now I fear nothing

And will love
Even a blade of grass
And Me.

THE GAPS

In the gaps
Between the apartments,
The cold wind blows, jealous of spring flowers.

Within human bodies
Living in the apartments
Buds also flower.

It is to these gaps that
Spring returns,
Finding even the caged

Humans are
Gaps

Where new things
Always begin.

Respect

Heaven rests
On the tops of poplars
And it
Merges into the trees.

You have to climb higher
To appreciate how high a mountain is.

My heart
Leaps joyfully and wildly
At the sight
Of a woman
And children.

The bud of the Cosmos
Shoots everywhere.

Love is
Respect

That spins the world smoothly
By placing others on high.

FLOWER-ENVYING COLD 1

I await
People in the spring.

To await someone,
Feeling the flow of my own blood
Inside me
Is a bitter joy,
And the cosmic dance

Is like
Mid-spring snow.

I await
People in the spring.

ILSAN POEMS 2

I'm alone
In white light.

The river flows
Far in the distance
Where summer clouds pass.

I look
And see death nearby.

Inside the depths
Of my heart,
A wind stirs

And I begin to walk
To meet it.

ILSAN POEM 4

Crickets
Sing throughout the night.

At their song my heart opens
And embraces the Universe.

Even in the dark, starless sky
I can see green stars

And hear
The sound of the river far away.

This autumn,
I may live without longing.

ILSAN POEMS 5

The flesh
On my body has departed.

I see only bones.

I dream of a rainbow
Inside these bones
On which the radiant white sun shines.

From the bones
Grass sprouts,
The sun and moon travel along their marrow.

Day and night
I hear the sound of shamans' songs.

The bones of the city,
The white bones of the streets,
My remnant bones,
All are places
Where a new heaven and earth grows.

INNER FLESH I

Mt. Chiak
Is dawning within me,
So I take a walk
Inside myself.
The clean I as well as the dirty I
Walk inside me,
Willingly changing leads,
While a chronic cough follows behind
Along this first snow-covered dusk road.

INNER FLESH 3

When the sun is about to rise
And the moon is sinking,
Stars are hard to find.

Neither the trace of my heart
Nor that of others is found easily.

In the midst of this vast world,
I think of life.

NOTHING

Out of desire, everything begins.

Out of hunger,
I
Loved you.

This afternoon,
When all insects and worms,
People on the street,
And the sun, moon and clouds are dying,

Love,
Cosmic and unknown,
Shoots out like the wind
From my empty heart.

Its fresh green
Startles me.

Out of desire
Everything is born.

LONELINESS

Lonely
Indeed.

Nothing is left
For me.

I embrace
The sun and moon,

The sick earth,
The lives of dying people,

And the feeble moans
Of the distant forest.

The laughter
Of my family
Is an unexpected gift.

A MEMORY

Once I touched her,
I could never forget
Her white skin.

Her skin is gone
But its white hue still lingers in the air.

It leads me to mountains,
To rivers blazing in the sun,
And to fields.

Finally it rests
In my heart

And burns
The night white.

EMPTY ROOM

My wife is
Gone.

The empty room
Is full of autumn.

The sky is blue.
The sun shines brightly.

The murmurs of people
Sound
And fade away

The universe nested today
In my empty heart.

Tonight,
I'm ready to die,

And, once dead,
I'll rise above the far-off river,
A crescent moon.

MY HOME

How far is it
From the mountaintop to the sun
Where You
Live?

The distance can be measured
Only by my longing.

There at night
The moon rises over the mountains
Amid my longing.

Beyond the stars
Lies the black hole of Stephen Hawking
And the baby universe,

And You are living over there
As humbly as a portulaca.

The faraway distance can be measured
Only by my longings

And You, the Cosmos,
Are the home
To which I shall return in the end.

THE SOUND OF RAIN

I close my eyes
And the sound of rain bathes me.

I hear
The rain,
Which falls from the sky and
Soars on back, after travelling to earth

With my ears open
I hear
The breath of all life,

The sighs of far-off trees
Which wither under acid rain,
The early winter rain
which trails a merciless cold.

My ears are wide open
To the sighs of all living things,
The sound of the soaring rain of bitter sighs,
And Yongsan shaman's chanting
Reverberate in my mind,
Wide like plantain leaves.

I hear
Its wild cry:
"Man,
What are you doing!"

CRICKET

At the cricket's song
A green star

Rests on
My rippling chest

And all creation in this strange city
On this autumn night
Is clothed in splendor.

AUTUMN TWILIGHT

Autumn twilight
Is sad to see

After everyone has gone
Home.

Withered sunflowers
Are traces of summers gone.

The sun blazes red,
Trailing long shadows.

Dusk in the field
And the moon in my heart.

Tonight I sleep
Holding the Universe in my heart.

A NEW CHURCH

When grass beckons
And soil and water shout
I
Go to church
After a long spell.

The church is on a mountain,
Open-walled
No roof.

Sun, moon and stars
Pray together here with me.
Comets come and stay
And the cosmos, across galaxy and nebulae,
Dances here

Women bare themselves
Naked, smile
And sing, shaking white handkerchiefs.

Are these allurements?

My
New church,
Church of grass, soil, and water,

New
Society of Jesus

Am I dreaming?

TO THE WEST[7]

In my heart
The flame subsides

In its place a white moon
Rises day and night

In this cold place
Even twilight fades

But flowers bloom
In dreams bad

And past remorse
Now melts into joys

Heaven rests
On an apricot leaf
Growing between the apartments

Come now
Beloved

And
Turn my black life
Into red budding flesh

On my way out
To the West.

THE THIRD PART

FIVE THIEVES

If you're gonna write poetry,
you should forget caution and write just like this.

It has been some time since I was spanked
in the torture room for my unrestrainable pen,
and I'm mad again to write something.
My body itches, tongue and hand, wild and restless.
And though my butt may burn from the flogging,
I've got to write
this unbelievably "true" story of thieves.

Since our nation was founded
at the foot of Bakdu Mountain on the third day of October
a long, long time ago,
they say an age as peaceful and happy
as the present never existed.
Behold! my belly button watches
and my butthole listens:
"Our Eastern nation is best,
enjoying peace and perfect happiness.
Where can we find the poor or thieves?
Well-fed farmers are wont to die over-fed,
and people live naked, tired of their silk clothes.
Though there is a thief like Jabong Ko,[8]
gangs rampaged even in Confucius' time.
Though corruption, graft and extortion are everywhere,
four rascals raged even in Yao and Shun's reign[9].
Virtuous kings and wise officers cannot do anything

about their thievish habits, but let them die."

And there lived five thieves
in downtown Seoul.
Their den at Tongbingo-dong is located high
upon the bank of the Han river.
It is built at the foot of a naked mountain,
bare as a plucked chicken-butt.
To the south it commands
a good view of the river,
where dung floats on the putrid water,
and to the north it boasts its magnificence
towards Sungbook-dong and Suyou-dong.
And, in between, a row of crowded shacks,
small as hermit-crab shells and dirty as boogers.
The five thieves built splendid flowery palaces
with high gates on Changchung-dong and Yaksoo-dong.
There, where the *kisang*[10] music never stops
and the sounds of cooking never cease,
is the very den of the notorious "Five Thieves,"
that sonuvabitch Plutocrat, sonuvabitch Aristocrat, sonuvabitch
Technocrat, sonuvabitch Autocrat,
and sonuvabitch Bureaucrat.
Their conceited heads are as big as Nam Mountain
and their necks as tough as Dongzhuo's navel.[11]

Unlike ordinary people
with five viscera and six entrails,
they have five viscera and seven entrails[12]
This seventh organ, as big as ox balls,
is the very home of their thievish habits.

Though they are disciples of one master,
their specialties vary.
By diligently practicing
day and night,
they have become grand masters of their skills.
And their businesses naturally prospered.
As their money grew their skills did, too.
One day, to celebrate their 10th anniversary
in business together
which had begun with a solemn blood oath,
they gather together
and agree to pit their finely-honed skills
against each other, with 100,000 kgs of
pure gold as the prize,
and place high a placard
on which is written "THEFT CONTEST."
It is a pleasant springtime
with a breeze and light clouds overhead.
All of them in turn boast of their secret skills,
dandily holding golf clubs in their hands.

The first contestant is
the sonuvabitch thief named Plutocrat.
Everything he has is decorated with gold:
he parades about in his gold clothes, gold hat,
gold shoes, gold gloves, gold watch,
gold ring, gold bracelets, gold buttons,
gold tie pin, gold cuff links, gold buckles,
gold teeth, gold fingernails, gold toenails,
gold zippers, and gold watch chains.

Announcing his appearance
with the poop-poop sound of farting
and shaking his sagging ass and huge pot-belly,
he totters out.
Hark and behold his skills.
He bribes ministers
and buys out vice-ministers
and handles them as easily as a cook kneads dough.
His favorite dishes are tax money, foreign loans,
and all preferential privileges and concessions,
and he swallows them
as if they were delicious delicacies
seasoned perfectly with vinegar, soy sauce,
mustard, hot pepper paste,
MSG, green onion, and garlic.
His favorite hobby is to keep concubines
and to beget children day and night.
By offering his numerous daughters
as concubines to men holding swords,
he easily winnows out top secrets.
Therefore all the best deals end up in his lap.
With only a $5 million bid he steals
something worth a $1 billion.
His favorite method of making money is
to buy deserted land cheap
and sell it for a fortune
when it begins to be developed.
His unwavering policy is
never to pay cash to his employees
but only lip service.
In sum, his talent in adapting himself

to circumstances surpasses that of Sunwukong[13]
and his butt-kissing skills
put even Chinese flatterers to shame.

The second contestant appears,
that sonuvabitch thief named Aristocrat,
muttering something in a phlegm-filled voice.
His back is as crooked as a hump,
and his narrow eyes are like
those of Chaochao.[14]
He is wrapping revolutionary pledges
all around his hairy body
and his hat and badge are also full of revolutionary pledges.

Unabashedly spitting thick phlegm
and waving a golf club as if it were a banner,
he thunders out his clichéd pledges.
Empty slogans flow from his forked tongue:
"It's time for revolution and change.
Change old evils into new ones,
Change unlawful money-making,
and make money-making itself unlawful,
Change illegal elections,
and make elections themselves illegal.
Modernize agriculture!
Poor farmers, give up farming!
Build! Remodel every house after
the crumbled down Wau Apartment[15]
Clean up society!
Follow thoroughly the example of Insook Chung,
the notorious high-class *kisang*.

Rise and rally for the sacred war of vote-buying.
Rise and stand up,
you Korean bank notes, Makkoli,[16]
hooligans, bums, pitted-faces, half-wits,
owls, badgers, shills, and you ghosts, too.
Sunzi's[17] famous military strategy teaches
that a true soldier should not dislike even evil ways.
Therefore politicians are by nature thieves
and public pledges are but empty words.
So step aside and keep away from me,
you dirty and ignorant commoners.
I'd rather play golf."

The third contestant appears,
that sonuvabitch thief named Technocrat.
His outward man is swollen like a balloon
and his eyes are as sharp as those of a viper.

His cold mien and tightly closed lips testify
that he is a clean-handed officer in every respect.
He shakes his head resolutely
and rejects "sweets,"
saying I don't eat "sweets" at all.
But, behold his back!
He has another face on his back.
It, knowing no abashment, laughs
and sends conciliatory smiles everywhere.
His teeth have rotted black,
having eaten too many "sweets."
His teeth are almost decayed away,
and he is sure to be a smelly, dirty-handed fellow.

Sitting lowly on high and highly on low
on his chair
as deep as a sea and as high as a mountain,
he oscillates between "Thank You, thank you "
and "No thanks, no thanks" all day long, doing nothing.
His way is to say "No, by no means" to realistic projects
and "Yes, no problem" to impossible ones.
On his desk lie huge files of paper
and under the desk lie bundles of bank notes.
He is a spaniel to his superiors and
a hound to his inferiors.
He makes a fortune by embezzling official money
and by openly asking for bribes.
Firmly denying what he has done,
he sings all day, instead
"White clouds, make sure my woman
isn't sleeping around on me."

The fourth contestant appears,
that sonuvabitch thief named Autocrat.
He is as tall as a utility pole
and the line of his soldiers is
as long as the Great Wall of China.
Having a hairy body, a badger's eyes,
a tiger mouth, a flat nose, and a long beard,
he is sure to be a beast in every aspect.
Medals of silver and gold,
pewter, bronze, and brass cover his whole body.
Overwhelmed by the weight of these decorations,
he creeps out on all fours
and displays his skill.

He steals soldiers' rice
and fills the empty bags with sand instead.
He gives just one or two cow hairs to his soldiers,
and eats all the meat by himself.
While his men, without barracks,
are freezing to death in the midwinter,
he forces them to build
his own big house with stolen wood and other materials.
His motto is
"Work hard until you sweat,
then you can overcome your cold."
His favorite items are trucks, clothes, fuels,
cooking materials, salaries,
and childern's small gifts for the soldiers.
His hobby is to beat runaway soldiers,
who leave camp out of hunger, nearly to death
for being ill-disciplined
and then throw them into prison.
He chooses the healthiest and strongest soldiers
and offers them to his wife
as sexual diversions,
while he practices his secret strategies
in the age old war between the sexes
with his own mistresses.

The last contestant appears,
that sonuvabitch thief named Bureaucrat.
Having waxy eyes suffering from cataracts,
his dirty face is beyond comparison.
But he looks around with glaring eyes,
while he controls the army

with his golf club in his left hand.

When he caresses his mistress' breasts
and writes slowly on them
"More produce, more exports, and more construction,"
she responds by saying
"Ah! oh! it tickles."
"Are you saying national affairs are
ticklesome, you ignorant bitch?"
Export more goods, even if we die of hunger.
Produce more goods, even if they don't sell.
Let's build a bridge over the Straits of Korea
with the bones of the people who starved to death
and have an audience with the Japanese gods.
Though music comes forth from his trumpet and drums,
his dark desire to pocket money oozes out
from the crevices of his instruments.
He owns a Mercedes Benz
in addition to his nice black sedan,
but uses the Corona[18] for public appearances
designed to display
his squeaky clean and humble nature.
His favorite method is to embezzle
large portions of the national budget
and take big bribes for awarding contracts.
And chewing gum to camouflage
his stinking "smell" is his hobby.
He, savoring his Kents, writes
on official papers in one stroke,
"Crack down on the use of foreign goods,"
and relishes his handwriting.

To the glib-tongued, half-mute reporters
who came to investigate his scandals,
he asks instead,
"What scandal on earth
can the Minister of State be involved in?"
and mutters some lines from a homecoming song
to vindicate his honorable poverty.
All of a sudden he changes his face
and invites them to a golf party,
asking them "What's your handicap?"

The ghosts who watched the contest
were scared to death by their dexterous skills
and desperately ran away,
fearing they would be robbed of their own bones.
That's why after the contest
there are not many
who offer sacrifices to the ghosts.

The contest heated up
as quickly as pumpkins ripen under the mid-autumn sun.
But in the midst of the heat
a stern royal order was issued
to immediately arrest the five thieves,
the shame of our nation.
It was so sudden and unexpected that
it was like thunder in a dry sky,
or the first frost of the season.
The police chief bows and promises to arrest
and bring them in immediately.
But, behold the police chief.

He has a pig's nose, a shaggy beard,
and a catfish muzzle on which
his spittle and the dregs of Makkoli dance.
His blood-thirsty ox eyes shake in their sockets busily,
and he roars like a lion and, in his haste,
dashes this way and runs that way,
while the big wen on his temple
swings up and down.
He watches every passerby with suspicion,
and begins to arrest them randomly.
In fact, he sweeps
every housefly, horsefly and dung-fly
rambling in Jongsam, Myongdong, Yangdong,
Mookyodong, Chungaechun, Tapsibri, and Wangsibri
into his big house,
and there he begins his sacred rite.

He usually orders the criminal
to kneel down on his knees
and then beats, hammers, strikes,
kicks, and treads him down mercilessly.
He pinches, bites, hurls, and throws him,
but it is a mere prelude
to his endless menu of tortures.
The next course is
to knock, break, bend, fling, screw, and wring them.
Then follows paring, stripping,
pushing needles inside his body,
and knocking him out.
His final course is
to make him pliable like a weeping willow

by scorching and screwing him until he keels.
To scare the flies to death,
he displays his many torture instruments:
a six-sided club, triangular iron poker, iron rake,
sword, dagger, saber, dirk,
rope for binding criminals, cudgel,
truncheon, whistle, bat,
rifle, machine gun, hand grenade,
tear bomb, smoke shell, vomit bomb,
dung bomb, piss bomb, muck bomb,
coal, and hard charcoal.

At his menacing words
which sound like a tiger's fart,
the shrivled folks shudder
and Kesoo, a poor farmer from Chulla-do,
quivers and shivers
as if he were attacked by the mid-winter cold in June.

"Shithead, aren't you one of the five thieves?"
"No, I am not."
"Then, who are you?"
"I'm a Pickpocket."
"Yes, yes. Aren't the fives thieves
Snatcher, Shoplifter, Pusher, Pickpocket, and Swindler?
You must be one of them."
"No, no, I'm not Pickpocket, then."
"Then who are you?"
"I'm Pimp."
"So, You're Pimp.
Aren't the five moral offenders

Pimp, Harlot, Whoremaster, Ruffian, and Pander?"
"Then, I'm not Pimp either."
"Then, who in the world are you?"
"I'm Gum-boy."
"Gum-boy, a-ha!
Gum-boy, Cigarette-Girl, Sock-Hawker, Drops-Peddler,
and Chocolates-Seller,
aren't they the five thieves who deal with foreign goods?"
"No, no, I"m not Gum-boy."
"Then who are you?"
"I'm a poor Beggar."
"Beggar, then you must be one of the five thieves,
because Beggar, Leper, Ragpicker, Gutter-snipe, and Panhandler are
the five thieves
who are most likely to commit crimes.
So imprison this rascal immediately."
"No, No, I'm not.
By god, I'm not one of the five thieves you seek.
I used to be a poor farmer
but came to Seoul to make money,
because I couldn't fill my own stomach through farming.
If I'm guilty of anything,
I'm guilty of stealing
just one piece of bread out of deathly hunger last night."

Then, the police chief begins to torture Kesoo.
He strikes, beats, and twists
Kesoo's legs and body like a screw.
And then he tempers, tans, and scorches him.
Turning him upside down,
he pours water into his nose

but later mixes it with hot pepper powder and vinegar.
But, in spite of all his efforts,
only the feeble cry of "No, I'm not "
crawls out from his mouth shamelessly.
The chief, at his wits' end,
changes his method and begins to console Kesoo:
"I'll save your neck
but only if you reveal
who the five thieves are and where they are."
Thereupon, Kesoo answers promptly
to save his life:
"The so-called five thieves are five beasts,
that sonuvabitch Plutocrat, sonuvabitch Aristocrat,
sonuvabitch Technocrat, sonuvabitch Autocrat,
and sonuvabitch Bureaucrat,
and now they're showcasing
their thieving skills in Tongbingo-dong."
"Um, their names sound familiar to me.
Are you sure they're beasts?"
"Of course they are. They're very cruel beasts indeed."
"Good, good, my son.
Why didn't you tell me that earlier?"
Happy to get this information,
the police chief hit his own knees,
but did it so hard that his knee bones split apart.
But he, enduring the deadly pain, urges
Kesoo to lead him to their den.
"To die is a personal matter
and to serve the nation is a public one.
By all means, I'll arrest them
and then put them to death by dismemberment.

That'll surely guarantee my promotion."

Look at the police chief as he follows Kesoo.
His glaring tiger eyes
like madly-spinning human headlights,
he dashes like a storm.
He thunders loudly,
"Step aside, make way for me,
otherwise you risk being one of the five thieves.
I am in a deadly hurry on my way to arrest them."
He jumps over Nam Mountain
in a single leap,
and lands in Tongbinggo-dong
with its magnificent view of the Han River.
With his stentorian voice and manly spirit,
he must be General Wan Lee[19] reincarnated.

Jumping into the contest arena,
the police chief cries loudly:
"Hark, you five beasts
You, cruel brutes, are you enjoying
such a sumptuous feast with the money
you screwed out of the poor commoners!
Now your feast is over.
Finally your debauchery has been heard up above
and I arrest you according to the royal order
for your bestial wickedness
and impairing the national honor."

Nobody listens to his words,
absorbed in their game instead.

Infuriated and amazed,
the chief begins to look around
and watches them carefully.
"They must be beasts,
but very splendid ones indeed.
I can hardly believe my own eyes
Is this real or just a dream?
If it's real, this must be heaven!"

Mighty dragon sculptures on the pillars
are ready to soar
and naked nymphs frolic
in the crystal clear swimming pool.
Their garden boasts miles of rare forest,
a garden tree worth a mllion *won*,
an imported dog worth a million *won*,
rare stones worth ten million *won*,
a stone lamp and a stone Buddha worth ten million *won*,
goldfish and carp worth a hundred million *won*,
and quails and sparrows worth a hundred million *won*.
In the den everything is automatic:
every door and wall opens automatically,
food and wine are served automatically,
and even flirting, wenching, and whoring are automatic.
A college graduate housemaid,
a Doctor of Economics accountant,
a Doctor of Forestry gardener,
a Doctor of Aesthetics hair dresser,
a Doctor of Business Administration steward
are working in the den.
Heating facilities are installed

to protect the lawn and birds from the cold,
and a cooling system in the pond
to protect fishes from the heat.
In order to keep the dog food fresh,
they put a refrigerator
in the dog villa.

Their den is a splendid combination
of Western and traditional architecture:
its roof is covered with traditional tiles
on a marble surface,
and its pillars are Corinthian
and its crossbeam, Ionic.
Fan-shaped angle rafters are decorated with iron engravings,
and the bottoms of the walls
are girdled with a golden sash.
Its vestibule is a glass room.
Its stone walls are decorated with arrowroot fabrics.
The front and back halls are wide open and
inbetween is located the main hall.
On the rooftop they built a second story
and decorated the building
with sliding lattice windows on which
the letter "Dao," signifying theft, is formed
from the ribs of the lattice.
Its lofty front and middle doors are Persian in style,
the bathroom modeled after a Turkish bath,
and the pigsty modeled with the Japanese in mind.
They dug a pool in the front yard
and built an artificial stone mound.
The police chief's head peeps through a chink

in the door into the den:
It has cabinets inlaid with mother-of-pearl,
sheenless steel chests,
dragon chests decorated with Chinese phoenixes,
phoenix chests decorated with dragons,
a chest with 3,333 drawers,
a bureau decorated with various flowers
including carnations,
a jade tray as big as a football field,
golden, silver, and bronze candlesticks
as tall as buildings,
an electronic grandfather clock, electronic bowls,
electronic kettles, electronic chopsticks,
electronic vases, electronic mirrors,
electronic books, electronic bags.
In addition to these electronics,
it has many rare and unheard of artifacts such as
stainless steel glass bottles, earthen wood bowls,
Chosun celadon, Koryo white porcelain[20],
a Picasso hung upside down, a Chagall pasted sidewise,
Sokpa orchids pressed within a golden frame,
400 hanging scrolls, 8,888 landscape and flower pictures.
The den also boasts pewter earthenware,
Tang vases, Japanese vases, American vases,
French vases, Italian vases,
a T.V. set encased in a tiger's hide,
a Sony cassette recorder in a stationary chest,
a Mitchell camera on a tortoise-shell desk,
an RCA camcorder in a coral bookcase,
a Parker fountain pen in an amber pencil case,
candle-lit chandeliers,

a standard lamp which burns castor oil.
Direct and indirect lighting shoots light
in angles that illuminate ceiling and floors
splendidly darkly richly scantily.

Hark and behold their women's ornaments:
They have blue jade hair pins, white jade shoe clasps,
golden breastpins, platinum teeth,
earrings with miniature paintings in them,
amber decorations accentuating their vulva,
coral ornaments hiding their buttocks,
ruby belly button adornments, sparkling amber buttons,
pearl earrings, noctilucent pearl nose rings,
amethyst necklaces, sapphire bracelets,
emerald ankle bracelets, diamond belts,
and turquoise sunglass frames.
But, ironically enough,
they wear gilt lead rings worth only three *won*
which shine
like torches in pitch-darkness.

At the rare and never-seen-before dishes
the police chief's mouth can't help but water.
This watering sound shakes the whole earth
like an earthquake.
They prepared cow hair barbecue,
roasted pig nose, fried goat beard, broiled buckhorn,
chicken legs cooked on a skewer,
dried pheasant fins, stewed sea bream wings,
salted toenails of crocker,
mixed raw fish dishes of sciaenoid, sea bass,

yellowtail, flatfish, and sweetfish ears,
hard-boiled small octopus and sea cucumber scales,
beef pork cutlet, pork beef cutlet,
bleeding swellfish bowels,
raw chestnuts, steamed chestnuts, apples,
dried pear seeds wrapped in gold foil,
sweet banana drink, pineapple punch,
and sugar-coated fig flower leaves.
Longart oil and honey pastry, fried methadone cake,
saccharine cookies, poached frog eggs,
green pea jelly, and agar cake are their desserts.

Their spirits are also numerous:
various flower and fruit spirits, Santory,
cinnamic alcohols, champagne, pine leaves spirits,
dry gin, purple shrimp spirit, ogalpi[21] alcohols,
Johnny Walker, Chinese matrimony vine alcohols,
White Horse, hermit spirits, Jim Beam,
cure-all spirits, Napoleon cognac, Makkoli,
rice wine, Korean gin, sake, hard liquors,
Chinese distiled liquors, vodka, and rum.

Almost out of his mind and broken-spirited,
the chief stares at these things, amazed,
and can hardly remember how to close his mouth.
His mouth watering
like a dog's on a hot summer's day, he exclaims,
"What a surprise this is!
All these are plunders from thieving?
Alas, Alas!
I should have been a thief myself earlier.

Those two damned words, 'Good Conscience,'
are my unforgivable, bitter enemy."
While he is wailing about his miserable lot,
one of the five thieves approaches him
and hands him a glass.
He had never heard of or seen the wine,
much less tasted it,
and it was so delicious and intoxicating
that he hastily drank two cups,
and then another two cups breathlessly.
As wet as a fish,
he stands up and makes an address.
Having chewed too much relish with the wine,
his teeth are almost ground away,
but the speech which comes from his trembling trap
is as grave and orderly as any sage's:
"Reverend thieves!
Thieving is not the crime of thieves,
but that of a society which breeds thieves.
Therefore, you respectable thieves
are diligent workers in our society.
So it's my earnest wish
that you devote yourselves to your sacred work,
do your best, and make grand progress."
While they are laughing
and clapping their hands loudly at the end of his speech,
he hooks Kesoo mercilessly
and binds him tightly.
"You, sonuvabitch,
I arrest you for your false accusation."

It is twilight,
and the sun is sinking in the West,
adding to the life-farer's loneliness.
A single goose looks for her companion
under the white, crescent moon,
and the river bleeds in the crimson twilight.
While a cuckoo cries and wails sadly,
the police chief burps and limps,
dragging Kesoo, dwindled to the size of a pea.
Alas, Alas!
Poor and miserable Kesoo,
my Kesoo,
You came to Seoul to earn a living,
unable to live in Chulla-do,
and you suffered every oppression and ill-treatment
in an unforgiving Seoul wherever you went.
What a nice destination
jail is for you!
But alas!
what can we do,
and who can stand up for you and deliver you
from such an unfair and ridiculous plight!
Farewell, Kesoo,
goodbye Kesoo,
please take care.

Immediately
Kesoo was thrown into the prison
and the five thieves,
appreciating the police chief's efforts,
appointed him doorkeeper of their den.

They did not forget to provide
his living facilities in a dog villa
just beside their lofty front door.
He was too happy at their munificence
and did his best with his many deadly weapons
to keep their den out of thieves' reaches.
He enjoyed a happy life in his dog villa for a while,
but on a bright sunny day
met a sudden death struck by a thunderbolt
while stretching himself.
And at that moment
the five thieves also dropped dead,
vomiting blood from their orifices.

This story has not been forgotten
but handed down from mouth to mouth
over a hundred generations,
and finally found its permanent place
in the lines of beggar poets
like me.

NOTES ON THE POEMS

1. The ocher road is a road on which the dead cross from this world to the next.

2. Around this time in the history of Korea wars were so frequent that it seemed there was a war every ten years or so.

3. The standard prison uniform in Korea.

4. A patch sewn onto the blue uniform of the criminal on which his number is embroidered.

5. Korean game cards on which various pictures are printed, similar to Tarot cards in the West

6. Alcoholic drink popular in Korea

7. The West here means the Pure Western World of Buddhism, which is similar to Paradise.

8. A notorious thief from the late 1960s in Korea. He once butchered a whole family with an axe.

9. The four notorious criminals in the age of Emperor Shun. In Chinese history, the age of Yao and Shun is generally regarded as the golden age.

10. A singing and dacing harlot of Korea.

11. Dongzho was a general of Wei and very fat. It is said that his body burned for three consecuitive days in cremation.

12. In Oriental medicine, an ordinary person has five viscera and six entrails. The five viscera are the liver, lungs, heart, kidneys, and spleen.

13. The main character in Wu Cheng En's novel, *The Journey to the West*. He is a monkey who is well known for his ability to transform himself into other shapes as he wishes.

14. A wicked hero who became a model for flatterers. Like other flatterers he is depicted as a man with small and narrow eyes.

14. An apartment building which collapsed in the late 1960s in Korea..

15. A traditional rice wine in Korea

16. A very famous author whose book, *Art of War*, has been regarded as one of the best Oriental books in its field.

17. The cheapest, smallest car once produced in Korea.

18. A famous general of Choson who fought against the foreign attackers.

19. Because celadons (Oriental pocelains bearing a translucent, pale green glaze) were produced during the Koryo Dynasty and white porcelains during the Choson Dynasty, Chosun celadon and Koryo white porcelain are factual impossibilities.

20. The root bark of Acanthopanax sieboldianus, which is used for medicinal purpose in the Orient.

WON-CHUNG KIM is currently a professor of English litera-ture at Hallym University in Chunchon, Korea. He earned his Ph.D. in English poetry at the University of Iowa in 1993. His main areas of research are ecological literature, ecological poetry and translation. He has translated the work of Hyonjong Chong (Trees of the World) and will soon publish an anthology of Korean ecological poets.

JAMES HAN is currently a full-time instructor of English con-versation and composition at Konyang University in Nonsan, Korea. He graduated from Pepperdine University with a B.A. in history and earned his J.D. at the State University of New York at Buffalo in 1994. He is presently working on his first novel.